THE PESTS
(LES FÂCHEUX)

Molière

*translated
slightly abridged and
adapted by*

Felicia Londré

BROADWAY PLAY PUBLISHING INC
New York
www.broadwayplaypub.com
info@broadwayplaypub.com

THE PESTS
© Copyright 2022 Felicia Londré

Cover photo by Brian Paulette

First edition: March 2022
I S B N: 978-0-88145-927-2

Book design: Marie Donovan
Page make-up: Adobe InDesign
Typeface: Palatino

This verse translation/adaptation as THE PESTS was first given a professional reading by Kansas City Actors Theatre on 7 March 2021.

Kansas City Actors Theatre premiered THE PESTS in a full production that ran 14-30 January 2022 at City Stage in Union Station. The cast and creative contributors were:

ÉRASTE .... Jake Walker
LA MONTAGNE .... J T Nagle
ORPHISE .... Weiyi Zhang
LYSANDRE & ORMIN .... Vi Tran
ALCANDRE .... Jerry Mañan
ALCIPE & LA RIVIÈRE'S GOON .... R H Wilhoit
ORANTE & LA RIVIÈRE .... Chioma Anyanwu
CLYMÈNE & LA RIVIÈRE'S GOON .... Christina Shafer
DORANTE .... Matthew Williamson
CARITIDÈS .... Robert Gibby Brand
MOLIERE, ALCIDOR & FILINTE .... Logan Black
MADAME DAMIS .... Jan Rogge

Director .... Matt Schwader
Choreography .... Ron Megee
Scenic design .... Dylan G Bollinger
Costume design .... Georgianna Londré Buchanan
Lighting design .... Mario Raymond
Sound design .... David Kiehl
Properties design .... Eric Palmquist
Fight choreography .... Logan Black
Dance Captain .... Christina Schafer
Stage Manager .... Adam M Fulmer
Assistant Stage Manager .... Pam West

ACKNOWLEDGEMENTS

Felicia Londré is especially grateful to John Rensenhouse, artistic chair of Kansas City Actors Theatre, director Matt Schwader, and the entire KCAT company for committing to a large-cast new play during the pandemic and taking extraordinary care to keep everyone safe throughout the production process and the three-week run.

The Board of Directors of KC MO*lière*: 400 in 2022 has worked steadfastly on all our Molière-related activities since June 2019 as we built up to Kansas City's public celebration of our playwright's 400th birthday on 15 January 2022. They are vice president Don Dagenais, treasurer Jim Weitzel, secretary Rebecca Smith, press & publications chair Patricia Hamarstrom Williams, Académie Lafayette liaison Dorothée Werner, higher education chair Jennifer Martin, and founding secretary Chantal Roberts, with special fond remembrances for our late founder Kip Niven and vice president Sarah Ingram-Eisner. Other invaluable associates are international relations chair Cyprienne Simchowitz, Alliance Française de Kansas City liaison Catherine Tissot, Mobile Molière director Stephanie Roberts, K-12 co-chairs Danielle Trebus and Martin English, administrative assistant Alexia Lamb, videographers Amanda Davison and John Rice, TARTUFFENTHROPE! playwright Philip blue owl Hooser and director Nathan Bowman, and super-volunteers Tracy Terstriep Herber, Fred Homan, and Gary Mosby. We are all supremely grateful to major donors Mark Edelman, Elisabeth Noble, Sieglinde Othmar, and the White-Simchowitz Family Charitable Fund.

Loving recognition as always goes to Venne-Richard Londré, my first reader and severest critic. Our daughter Georgianna Londré Buchanan not only designed the delightful costumes for THE PESTS but she also created the mascot-head MoMo whose presence has enlivened so many of KC MO*lière*: 400 in 2022's events.

TRANSLATOR'S NOTE

In the course of the nonprofit KC MO*lière*: 400 in 2022's three-year build-up to Kansas City MO's city-wide celebration of its 200-year French heritage along with Molière's 400th birthday (15 January 2022), I reread many of Molière's plays both in French and in translation. I was shocked to discover that LES FÂCHEUX, the charming trifle that skyrocketed Molière into his career-defining relationship with the king, was not readily available in an English translation other than the prose version attributed to Thomas Shadwell (c. 1642-1692) and titled THE BORES.

In an idle moment, I played around at translating the opening scene into rhyming couplets. Lacking credentials other than my hobby of memorizing poetry (currently around 175 poems active in my brain with Robert Service and Jean de La Fontaine at the head of the pack), I expected no return on my effort and set it aside as more pressing demands took over. A few months passed. On a whim I showed the trial pages to my husband. Surprisingly, he encouraged me to continue and I finished a draft during that first pandemic summer 2020. The bimonthly online Molière book club read it and offered insightful suggestions. John Rensenhouse, artistic director of Kansas City Actors Theatre, read it and put together a professional reading on Zoom and YouTube as a benefit for KC MO*lière*: 400 in 2022; it garnered $575 in donations! The enthusiasm of the cast and the audience led the KCAT board to consider full production once theatres were allowed to re-open.

The play is usually referenced in English writing on Molière as THE BOORS or THE BORES. Neither struck me as a ticket-selling translation of the title (although I never dreamed that ticket selling would be a concern for my labor of love). I chose THE PESTS partly because it's a fairly useful rhyme word. My guiding principle of translation was to make a fun and playable text while respecting Molière's intentions. I admire Richard Wilbur's brilliant renderings of English rhymed couplets that exactly match up line-by-line with Molière's French. In choosing to adapt, rather than to translate in Wilbur's mode, my idea was to tighten up the long speeches; that is, to translate each long speech as a whole rather than as individual lines. An unexpected result of my approach was that I began to allow very subtle contemporary resonances to creep into the vocabulary. One actor commented after the first read-through that his two favorite words in the script were "performative victimhood." In production, it felt right that these tiny occasional liberties accelerated toward the culminating "beer and barbecue" in the final scene.

To have the superb Kansas City Actors Theatre produce my translation was beyond anything expected from a translator's labor of love. Moreover, KCAT set opening night for the evening of 15 January 2022, to follow the huge public celebration of Molière's 400th birthday at the Nelson-Atkins Museum of Art. The museum, short-staffed due to Covid illnesses, found it necessary to postpone the birthday celebration to 1 May, but THE PESTS opened as scheduled, while KCAT took every precaution and successfully completed the run with no illness in the cast or crew.

This classic piece worked beautifully thanks to the company's ability to convey truthfulness in hilarity.

Because director Matt Schwader and choreographer Ron Megee so brilliantly mined the text for clues to physical action, I include in square brackets some indications of what worked well in the KCAT production. For example, one can read the dialogues between Éraste and his valet La Montagne as a standard seventeenth-century master-servant relationship. Yet J T Nagle's La Montagne, while not quite defying the norms of deference to his master, emerged as a cleverly assertive persona. The payoff to their mutual chafing came with Matt Schwader's touch of directorial genius: he brought La Montagne back onstage to save the day in the fight scene. His blocking left Éraste disarmed and facing the three members of the La Rivière gang when La Montagne suddenly reappeared and distracted La Rivière.

Another production liberty that worked despite my initial misgivings was to change Orphise's guardian Damis to a guardian aunt, and I have changed the pronouns in this script accordingly. Clad in formidable layers of black satin, Jan Rogge established a powerful presence when she stepped through the doorway. Her pratfall, when attacked by La Rivière, always elicited laughter at the flailing legs in ruffled white bloomers amid white crinolines.

Molière's LES FÂCHEUX was originally performed in the landscaped gardens at Vaux le Vicomte on 17 August 1661 as part of the festivities offered by Nicolas Fouquet in honor of Louis XIV. The festive evening marked Molière's rise to royal favor and Fouquet's tragic downfall, but that's another story….

Finally, as a bit of context for the opening dance, here is a brief description that draws from documents of the period to show how that preliminary sequence was done on 17 August 1661:

As soon as Molière left the stage, twenty jets of water shot into the air like dancing fountains. A rock split open and there was a Naïad—played by Molière's gorgeous red-headed leading lady Madeleine Béjart, scantily clad as a goddess.

Several eye-witness accounts tell us that it was an astonishing moment when the 43-year-old actress appeared from the rock, looking like a maiden in the bloom of youth. She spoke a few verses—written by the host's general manager Pelisson—in praise of the king. The poem included these lines:

If our king commands it, even statues can move.
Nymphs and satyrs, join us here in this grove.

At that moment, the garden statues came to life. They were dancers who had been perfectly immobile until then. Satyrs and nymphs popped out from behind the trees and danced while the Naïad finished the poem, evoking the harmony of nature and the social order. Then the dancers and musicians left the scene and the play began.

CHARACTERS

(phonetic pronunciation in parentheses, although most names are never spoken in the dialogue)

ÉRASTE, *a Marquis (mar-KEE) tormented by pests* (Ay-RAHST)

LA MONTAGNE, *his valet* (La-mohn-TAHN-yeh)

ORPHISE, *the object of* ÉRASTE'*s love* (or-FEEZ)

ALCIDOR, *non-speaking* (Ahl-SEE-dohr)

LYSANDRE, *fancies himself a composer/choreographer* (Lee-SAHN-druh)

ALCANDRE, *a would-be duellist seeking a second* (Ahl-KAHN-druh)

ALCIPE, *a card-player* (Ahl-SEEP)

ORANTE, *coquette, argues for emotional restraint* (Awh-RAHNT)

CLYMÈNE, *coquette, argues for jealous passion* (klee-MEN)

DORANTE, *has a mania for horses and hunting* (doh-RAHNT)

CARITIDÈS, *a self-inflated scholar* (kah-ree-tee-DESS)

ORMIN, *a financial wheeler-dealer* (or-MANH)

FILINTE, *an overly-earnest friend* (fee-LANT)

MADAME DAMIS, *aunt/guardian of* ORPHISE (mah-DAHM dah-MEE)

LA RIVIÈRE, (Lah-REE-vyehr)

Two GANG MEMBERS, *non-speaking, but growls, grunts, and "aaarghh" will be liberally added by actors*

Prologue

(Sound of chattering and then applause. MOLIERE *enters, wearing street clothes, and addresses the audience, notably Louis XIV, who is presumably seated at center amid the courtiers assembled in the garden at Vaux-le-Vicomte. The performance space is surrounded by hedges and includes stone garden benches. Sculptures and fountains are optional.)*

MOLIERE: Merci, merci. C'est moi, Molière.

Here I am in street clothes, humbly addressing Your Majesty the King and hoping this trifle may be worthy of his attention.

Never was a theatrical presentation geared up more hastily than this one. Can you believe that a complete comedy was imagined, written, memorized, and pulled together in two weeks?! I'm not upset or anything. I just wanted you to understand that this is not going to be standard comedy format.

The subject is obnoxious people—pests. We all know dozens of types of annoying people, both at court and in town, but I had to hold back and pick just a few of them. Even at that, there wasn't time to fit them into a plot with the usual intrigues, so I decided to let these characters just be themselves. And I hope they are the ones that this illustrious gathering will find most amusing.

Oh, I'd love to write like one of the great tragic poets! Well, yes, I coulda been a contender who cites Aristotle and Horace. Another time, perhaps.

But I do need to say something about the musical eruptions that punctuate this comedy. The plan was to present a comedy and a ballet. But in the time allotted we couldn't get a sufficient number of excellent dancers that would allow some to keep a dance sequence going while others changed their costumes. The solution was to sandwich the ballet entrées between the acts of the comedy.

We tried to fit the themes of the various entrées to the action of the play, and… so… Some work better than others. The point is that this is something new for theatre in our own time. I suppose we could credit Aristophanes and his use of a chorus. We might get back to antiquity in the future.

For right now, as Your Majesty's faithful subject, I make my exit and leave before your eyes the splendid vision of this garden paradise.

(Opening dance sequence inspired by aspects of the outdoor performance at Vaux le Vicomte on 17 August 1661 when classical garden statues came to life as baroque dancers and 43-year-old Madeleine Béjart emerged—like a Venus from a seashell—to flaunt her assets under minimal drapery:)

[In Ron Megee's chorography, the up center hedges part just enough to reveal the silhouette of a courtier flanked by fluttering blue draperies. To strains of baroque music, the courtier dances to center while the blue chiffon continues its undulation by unseen hands. From the wings, a portable hedge is wheeled onstage. The dancer traipses over to the hedge and rotates it to reveal a modern electronic sound board. He tries on the headset with a flourish and tackles the keyboard. The sound abruptly switches to hip hop. Puzzled-looking dancers appear in the opening and soon get caught

up in the rhythms. The two with blue chiffon attached to fans dance into the playing area followed by a motley assortment of extra dancers. Then a small platform is wheeled through the hedge gap to center stage; it carries a middle-aged woman in pinkish gold lamé drapery; she stands unsteadily in front of a large gold seashell painted on the backing. Once the platform is in place, she turns on the charm and blows kisses to the audience. A lighted sign above her head begins flashing: THE PESTS. The dancers are improvising to the contemporary sounds when suddenly ÉRASTE *steps into view and everything comes to a halt. The dancers scurry to remove the sound board hedge and the wheeled platform, leaving the stage to him and his valet.]*

ACT ONE

ÉRASTE: *(He might be peripherally addressing his valet, but neither actor nor character can ever forget that Louis XIV is the one audience member that matters.)*
Now why on earth must I be so oppressed
By a human species, the irrepressible pest?
Wherever I go, the pests accost me and employ
Their personally witless ways to annoy.
But the pest who pestered me just now today
Was by far the worst: he massacred the play!
Let me tell you what he did; I need to vent.
At the comedy I'd hoped for merriment.
I'd bought a place on stage, an excellent seat.
The ingenue listened to the hero entreat—
Then the pest barged in late and brashly pushed his
  way
Right up onto the stage; it stopped the play.
Coat panels fluttering, he called for a chair
And planted it down center, exactly where
It blocked the view of half the audience!
Good heavens, don't the French have any sense?
His ribboned doublet was overly festooned
Like the critical comments he quite loudly crooned.
The actors went on bravely as best they could,
But the pest spotted me, and like a block of wood,
Helpless and red-faced, I wished I dared to flee.
Approaching me and bellowing "My dear marquis,"
He carried on his one-sided conversation,

Not heeding my diplomatic indication
That the show was very good and merited attention.
He saw it last week, he said, going on to mention
How he offered his critique to the great Corneille
Who always sought his advice when writing a play!
This type of pest targets men of title or renown
And acts familiar with them while ignoring their
    frown.
Scene by scene he told me what plot twist would come
    next
While I squirmed and the players tried not to look
    vexed.
The play ended at last; I dashed for the door,
But the pest persisted, bragged of his honors and more
Like his standing at court (I'm sure that's news to you)
And suggested we ride together for all to view.
Still to be polite, I said a friend expected me to dine;
He said: "Any friend of yours is a friend of mine!
So I'll join you and add my glamor to your table."
I felt trapped and doomed and totally unable
To shed this pest. But luckily just then
A magnificent carriage with fancy footmen
Pulled up near us. Its aristocratic crest
Turned the toadying head of my awful pest.
And that distraction let me escape and come here,
Hoping not to miss Orphise, whom I revere.

LA MONTAGNE:
Monsieur, if that's the worst thing in your life,
You're not so badly off. All men face strife.
Without such pests we might be too happy on earth.
With irritations like that, our pleasures have more
    worth.

ÉRASTE:
Well, bad as that pest was, there's another even worse:
Madame Damis, her aunt, does all she can to reverse

My efforts to see Orphise. Did she thwart us anew?
For now it's long past time for our rendez-vous.

LA MONTAGNE: Oh, girls are like that. The cute ones
   don't live by clocks.
Just relax and she'll get here, I'll bet my socks.

ÉRASTE:
It's true and yet I tremble, for I love to such extent
That a molehill becomes a mountain in every event.

LA MONTAGNE: If your love is so perfect that her trifles
   seem like crimes,
Shouldn't she turn the tables on you sometimes?
And blow off your big worries like lighter than air?

ÉRASTE: But does she love me? Does she even care?

LA MONTAGNE:
What? How can you doubt the love that she declared?

ÉRASTE:
But did it equal the ardor of the heart that I bared?
An overheated heart wants repeated assurance.
It fears declarations that might lack endurance.

LA MONTAGNE:
Sir, I see your neck-ruffle has come all undone.

ÉRASTE: Never mind.

LA MONTAGNE: You'd look a mess for her, your
   honey-bun?
Let me make this small adjustment in it.

ÉRASTE: You're choking me!

LA MONTAGNE: Hold on till I pin it.

ÉRASTE: Aaaaghhh! You pricked me!

LA MONTAGNE: A touch of the comb just here—

ÉRASTE:
Clumsy oaf! You and your comb could slice off an ear!
To comb oneself in company is now quite the fashion.

LA MONTAGNE:
All I wanted to do was to make you look dashin'.
Now by your grace, may I brush the dust off your hat?

ÉRASTE: Stand apart from me then, if you must do that.

LA MONTAGNE:
Shake-shake-shakin' the dust away. Shake-shake—

ÉRASTE:
Hurry up, will you? Oh, such a bother you make!

LA MONTAGNE:
Shake-shake! Shake-shake! Every last little bit of dust—

ÉRASTE: That's enough! Give it back. You've quite
   finished, I trust?

LA MONTAGNE:
I'm shaking it clean so you'll be all spic and span.
Shake-shake!

ÉRASTE: Stop that—flicking it like a fan!
Must I slap you? If I do, it will be hard enough to hurt.

LA MONTAGNE:
Here, sir. Ooops! I dropped it in the dirt.
Let me just give it a few shakes more—

ÉRASTE:
Enough! You've made it even worse than before.
A plague on all valets! If only we didn't need 'em,
I'd send him packing for good and enjoy my freedom.

(Enter ORPHISE and ALCIDOR.)

ÉRASTE:
There she is! My Orphise, the epitome of charm!
But who's that man? And they're walking arm in arm!

(ÉRASTE bows to her, but she keeps walking and turns her
head away from him. ORPHISE and ALCIDOR exit.)

[ALCIDOR pauses at the exit, looks back, and says "Ooh, la,
la!"]

ÉRASTE: What's this? It's our appointed meeting place,
But she ignores me and turns away her face!
Am I dreaming? Oh, tell me it's not true she looked
   away—

LA MONTAGNE: Monsieur, I must shut up, since I'm a
plague-cursed valet.

ÉRASTE: So you are if you won't help me figure this out.

LA MONTAGNE: I'm too smart to provoke a slap on the
snout.

ÉRASTE:
My heart is torn apart, it's bleeding, it's quaking,
And I need another viewpoint—

LA MONTAGNE: I can do shaking.

ÉRASTE: You'll do as I say. You must follow my
   beloved Orphise.
Find out what she's up to—

(LA MONTAGNE *starts to go, but turns back.*)

LA MONTAGNE: —and if she has a new squeeze?

ÉRASTE: And report back to me as quickly as you can.

(LA MONTAGNE *starts to go, but turns back.*)

LA MONTAGNE:
So I watch what she does—but what about the man?

ÉRASTE: Him also. Now go!

(LA MONTAGNE *starts to go, but turns back.*)

LA MONTAGNE: Do I let them see me or no?

ÉRASTE:
If they question you, tell them that I wanted to know—
Since I'm waiting for her—just when she plans to
   show.

(LA MONTAGNE *starts to go, but turns back.*)

LA MONTAGNE:
You'll be here in this very spot when I return?

ÉRASTE:
Yes! Now go or I'll kick you to hell where you'll burn!

(LA MONTAGNE *exits.*)

ÉRASTE: No wonder I was earlier so full of anxiety.
This missed meeting has erased my self-propriety.
No sooner my heart had leaped up at her sight
She quashed it like a foot on a lowly termite.

[LYSANDRE's *ruffled arm appears above the hedge as he calls
"Woo-hoo! Marquis!".*]

(*Enter* LYSANDRE.)

LYSANDRE:
Seeing you from afar, dear Marquis, I came winging,
Knowing that you above all can appreciate my singing.
And with your supreme taste in music, I'm pleased to
    share
My latest composition, a delicate air.
They're humming at court my little confection
And vying with verses to enhance its perfection.
So my musical fame spreads. None can come near it.
I see, dear Marquis, you can hardly wait to hear it.
(*He hums a tune.*)
Now is that not enchanting?

ÉRASTE: Ah.

LYSANDRE: Just listen again.
Your good opinion will make me the happiest of men.
(*He croons several more times.*)
Tell me now what you think.

ÉRASTE: Oh, very nice.

LYSANDRE:
And some dance steps I've created add the extra spice.
You take the woman's part and let me demonstrate.

(LYSANDRE *sings, speaks, and dances, leading* ÉRASTE *to
follow in the female dancer's role.*)

LYSANDRE:
Note my footwork. You follow me—but not so sedate.
I offer my arm, incline my head, a little note of grace.
She turns and voilà. We end up face to face.
(After he ends his demonstration:)
Your verdict, dear Marquis?

ÉRASTE: You've demonstrated admirably.

LYSANDRE:
I worked it out myself. No dance instructor for me.

ÉRASTE: So I see.

LYSANDRE: And my steps—?

ÉRASTE: Clearly yours alone.

LYSANDRE: Let me lead you again and then you'll make
   them your own
Since we're friends—

ÉRASTE: You must excuse me for now,
I'm expected elsewhere, if you'll allow…

LYSANDRE:
Another time, when you wish; we'll add the lyrics.
Oh-ho, just you wait till the foot and the ear mix—

ÉRASTE: I can hardly wait.

LYSANDRE: Meanwhile off I go to find master Lully.
The genius of my floor pattern he will see truly
Along with the song and its *je ne sais quoi*.
Then I'll win the gaze of great Louis *le roi*.
(He exits singing.)

ÉRASTE:
Oh, heavens! it's hard to remember *noblesse oblige*
When idiots like that have us always under siege.
My position calls for niceties in response to nonsense.

Between my thought and my speech I put up a high
  fence.

(Enter LA MONTAGNE.*)*

LA MONTAGNE:
Sir, Orphise is coming; she said goodbye to that guy.

ÉRASTE:
Oh! my mind's a mixed-up mess, I don't know why.
One glance at her beauty and my heart will capitulate
Though my reason tells me there's reason to hate.

LA MONTAGNE:
Your reason, monsieur, is scarcely quite reasonable.
Your heart is surely not so *(Pause to find a rhyme)*
  unseasonable
As to form a judgment before the lady says hello.
So calm down, tame your impulse, don't bellow.

ÉRASTE: Yes, of course, a courtly man's composure
Best camouflages anger's rash exposure.

(Enter ORPHISE.*)*

ORPHISE:
Oh, my, what an unwelcoming look on your face
To greet my arrival at our appointed place!
Is something troubling you? Oh, what a big sigh
You heaved when you saw me, Éraste! Why?

ÉRASTE: Alas! can you be so cruel as to pretend
You don't know how you hurt me and send
My spirits into a tailspin of despair
When you walked by me just as if you didn't care?
While some other gentleman held your gaze—

ORPHISE: *(Laughing)*
And that's what caused you to look half-crazed?!

ÉRASTE:
You laugh at my suffering, my human weakness?
To comprehend what I saw, my freak guess

Was that you must have found a new flame,
Leaving me to wither in heartbroken shame.

ORPHISE: Oh, yes, I have to laugh at something so trite.
I shouldn't stoop to explain, but all right—
The gentleman you saw was a bore and a pest,
But has strong ties at court, so I tried my best
To be pleasant and I let him escort me
To my carriage, so it could transport me
Round the garden to the other gate.
And here I am, not even very late!

ÉRASTE:
Oh, Orphise, can your hasty words halt my fear?
Is your heart—to match mine—well and truly sincere?

ORPHISE:
Didn't I just explain what you wanted to know?
Are you trying to deal me yet another blow?
If you persist with this foolishness, farewell—

ÉRASTE: Don't be angry! Can't you see I'm in hell?
Orphise, all you've told me repays my devotion,
My heart's enflamed and drowned in an ocean
Of tears in torments that I well deserve.
Love me and never again will I swerve—

ORPHISE: Methinks the gentleman protests too much,
But I—

(*Enter* ALCANDRE.)

ALCANDRE: Pardon, Monsieur, I must be such
A boor as to speak with you confidentially.
Pardon, madame, it's between him and me.

(ORPHISE *exits.*)

ALCANDRE:
My dear Marquis, may I prevail on your benevolence?
There's a man over there who's given me offense.
He said some words to me that made me feel bad,

So I see no recourse but to challenge the cad.
But to fight a duel I need a second—

ÉRASTE: *(Thinks for a moment before speaking)*
I beg pardon, Vicomte, your score must be reckoned
Without me, without the aid of my well-honed sword.
Fourteen years I served and as soldier ran toward
The most dangerous spots to fight for the king.
He has outlawed dueling and I will not bring
Dishonor to his decree. Therefore, I choose
To obey my sovereign, while you I refuse.
For any honorable designs, my dear Vicomte,
You may call upon me and I will be prompt.
By my frankness I hope you will not be offended.
For now, dear Vicomte, our conversation is ended.

*(*ALCANDRE *exits.)*

*[*ALCANDRE *draws as if to take on the offstage offender, but startles, turns, and runs offstage in the opposite direction.]*

ÉRASTE:
To the devil with such pests! Now where is Orphise?

LA MONTAGNE: Monsieur, I think she's—
(He points in all directions.)

ÉRASTE: Go find her, if you please!
Try that path, and that one, seek in every direction.
I'll wait till you return with my precious pretty
     perfection.

(ACT ONE ballet)

First Entrée

(Croquet players invade the space and cause ÉRASTE *to step aside.)*

(After they finish their dance, he returns to wait for ORPHISE.*)*

Second Entrée

(*Curious about* ÉRASTE, *dancers surround him and look him over, until he again retires to one side.*)

[*In Ron Megee's choreography, the music and movement switched back and forth between slow-motion baroque and strong-beat hip hop. In slow motion, the characters enter, each carrying a croquet mallet while another spins the round shape of a tiny parasol as if it were the ball. They pantomime hitting the ball and sending it spinning to another player to hit.* ÉRASTE *walks among them as if invisible. He exits and the rhythmic beat takes over. Somehow each dancer suddenly carries two mallets, now used with crossed arms and clacking sounds. The dance is interrupted by the sound of thunder and rain. The "croquet ball" becomes an umbrella as all run to exit the stage.*]

END OF ACT ONE

ACT TWO

(ÉRASTE *enters, holding out his palm to test whether the rain has ceased.*)

ÉRASTE:
A rain of pests is worse than raining cats and dogs.
I hope that shower drove them back into their bogs.
Luckily the summer storm has quickly blown away
And spared the court's brocades and gold lamé.
But now the sun is sinking; where is my valet?
Where's my Orphise? She went astray—is she okay?

(*Enter* ALCIPE.)

ALCIPE: Hello there!

ÉRASTE: Not another one! Oh, heaven forfend!
By thunder! This rain of pesky interlopers has no end.

ALCIPE:
Well met, dear Marquis, I'm bursting to explain
How I lost at piquet while sheltered from the rain.
You know, of course, how I excel at piquet.
So I enticed my weaker would-be rival to play
By giving him a handicap—twice the fifteen
That's the norm. When you see him preen
About winning, please take my part.
I held the ace, king, jack, and ten of heart
Plus the ace of spades, the king and queen of clubs.
You follow me? Now here's the part that rubs:
I discard, I draw—another heart!—the queen!
So if only I had not doubled the fifteen….

But he laid out six spades, smirked, and cried "Pic!"
So flabbergasted was I, I couldn't speak.
When two points was all that I would need to win—

ÉRASTE:
Card-playing inevitably brings chagrin; it's built in.

ALCIPE:
It came down to which to keep, which to discard,
A choice, as you know, in piquet, can be hard.
The points as we play I constantly calculate
In my mind, and it's my points that ought to escalate.
But this time—

ÉRASTE: Sir, I've followed each move in your story
And assure you that this cannot detract from your
     glory.
None of this can undermine your well-known merits.

ALCIPE: And yet it will ever weigh down my spirits.
If only the ace of spades I hadn't discarded—

ÉRASTE: Now if you'll excuse me, the time is far sped
When I must take leave—

ALCIPE: *(Starts to exit, then stops.)*
                              Only two points! Only two!
(Exits)

ÉRASTE: So many pests are swarming—what can I do?
But here comes my valet, the slowest type of pest.

(Enter LA MONTAGNE.*)*

LA MONTAGNE:
Forgive me, Monsieur, I've truly tried my best.

ÉRASTE:
But where's Orphise? You were sent to fetch her.

LA MONTAGNE:
I ran round and round. She's a tough one to catch, Sir.

ÉRASTE: Yes, yes, but what news?

LA MONTAGNE: I found her, but then she—

ÉRASTE: She said what? She has a message for me?

LA MONTAGNE:
You want to know exactly what she said?

ÉRASTE: Out with it—even if it's something I dread.

LA MONTAGNE:
Hold on and I'll tell you, but I'm all out of breath—

ÉRASTE:
Villain! Are you attempting to hasten my death?

LA MONTAGNE:
Yes, your sweetheart gave me some words to relay.
I see you're impatient for what I'm supposed to say,
But it wasn't easy for me, all that running around—

ÉRASTE: Devil take you! Your digressions confound—

LA MONTAGNE: You've read Seneca; you should
    moderate your passion.

ÉRASTE:
Seneca from you! Watch your head before I bash in—

LA MONTAGNE: Your Orphise says— Wait! You've got
    an insect on your coat.

ÉRASTE: No matter.

*[In his impatience, ÉRASTE plucks the insect from LA
MONTAGNE's hand and eats it.]*

LA MONTAGNE:
                She said—if you'll just listen and take note.

ÉRASTE: She said what?

LA MONTAGNE: You know her, can't you guess?

ÉRASTE: *(Aside)* I must stay calm—if that's the way to
    make him confess.

LA MONTAGNE: Her message is that she wishes you
    would wait for her here.

*[Enunciating each word between "she" and "here" with a
pause between each word while* ÉRASTE *seethes but restrains
himself.]*

LA MONTAGNE:
It won't be long before she gets away and can appear.
Meanwhile she's detained unavoidably
In a brief encounter with people of quality.

ÉRASTE:
Very well. I'm happy to think on her while I wait
In this spot she has chosen. I can meditate
On some verses for a tune I know she finds pleasin'
As my heart restores a balance with my reason.

(Enter ORANTE *and* CLYMÈNE.*)*

*[*ÉRASTE *sees them and hides behind* LA MONTAGNE.*]*

ORANTE: Everyone we know will embrace my side of it.

CLYMÈNE: We'll soon see about that. Just abide a bit—

ORANTE: My reasons are already known and accepted.

CLYMÈNE: Under our sovereign, all views are protected.

[When the women glance upstage, LA MONTAGNE *steps
aside so that* ÉRASTE *is revealed, cowering.]*

ORANTE:
Ah! here is one who can see the bigger picture:
Let's submit the case to him *sans* constricture.
Marquis, if you please, may we call upon you
To judge a question that's arisen between us two?
It's an issue that divides us as we mull it over:
What trait constitutes the perfect lover?
We hold contrary views and neither will budge.

ÉRASTE:
On that subject, I am far from being the best judge.

ORANTE:
Not at all! Your wit is celebrated and your reputation—

ÉRASTE: I beg you—

ORANTE:
    It's settled! Clymène and I accept your arbitration.

CLYMÈNE:
You'll bring your experience of what is right and just
And you'll choose the truth of my views, I strongly
    trust.

ÉRASTE: *(Aside)*
This is when I wish for a more cunning valet,
One who could find an excuse to call me away.

[LA MONTAGNE *has retreated upstage with a book. He*
waves cheerily when he hears the word "valet", but does not
stir from his spot.]

ORANTE:
I know the Marquis and I'm not the least bit stressed
About the choice he'll make when my points are
    pressed.
Now here's the issue on which we both wax zealous:
Should the ideal lover be—or not be—jealous?

CLYMÈNE:
That's to say, does the beloved find more engaging
A cold fish or one with jealous passions raging?

ORANTE:
A calm demeanor is not the same as a cold fish!

CLYMÈNE: But a tormented lover is exquisitely delish!

ORANTE:
Allowing access by others shows greater respect.

CLYMÈNE:
The ardor that brooks no rival is the one I'd elect.

ORANTE: Jealousy's an aberration on a par with hatred.
It will turn against itself just as spite fed
By spite will seek evidence of crime
And guilt will taint a pure innocence over time.

Tolerance for all makes true love more splendid
Than the ranting lover who seeks to be offended.
If the lover needs rivals to stir up his emotion,
He'll turn into a bore when there's no commotion.
Better far is interaction on an even keel
For meeting of minds: that's the love that's real.

CLYMÈNE: Clearly you've not been wooed by courtly
    milquetoasts,
So stand-offish and poised, they might as well be
    ghosts.
They're too cowed to come forward and declare a
    belief;
If love is stolen from them, they befriend the thief.
Can one even detect a heartbeat in their chests,
Those passive galants, those weaklings, those—

ÉRASTE: Pests?!

CLYMÈNE: Houseguests—in a heart that should be
    forcibly occupied,
Held hostage to the conqueror, all ransom denied.
An exciting lover is forever suspicious
Of my flirtations. If his transports become pernicious,
The vehemence of apologies displayed in equal
    measure
Along with some weeping—that's my source of
    pleasure.

ORANTE:
If performative victimhood is what gives you a high,
I can send you some professional plaintiffs to try—
Actors who know how to tear a passion to tatters,
Since the show before a public to you is what matters.

CLYMÈNE:
If you're so prudish you fear displays of passion,
Enjoy your ivory tower. Your demeanor's quite out of
    fashion.

ORANTE: I'll stay the course, hold out for mutual trust,
A partnership less prone to falter and go bust.
You've heard our arguments and now, dear Marquis,
What's the verdict? Which is the stronger plea?

ÉRASTE: As an unwilling judge, I must hesitate to say...
Both cases have points that might readily sway
A jury's verdict. Can we call it a match? or a truce?

ORANTE:
But we haven't even moved from love to deuce!

(ORPHISE *enters opposite and watches what appears to be
a compromising situation between* ÉRASTE *and the two
women.*)

ÉRASTE:
Another court will surely give scope to your game.
Take your case elsewhere.

(As ORANTE *and* CLYMÈNE *exit:)*

ORANTE: Well now, that's a shame!

ÉRASTE: *(Seeing* ORPHISE*)*
You've come at last! I was beginning to wonder—

ORPHISE:
No, I mustn't interrupt. I wouldn't steal your thunder.
You were deeply occupied with your clever company,
Who clearly merit more attention than little old me.

ÉRASTE:
You've no idea how agonizingly I was employed.
You reproach me for something I could not avoid?
But let's not—

ORPHISE: Let me go. I'll not obstruct your way
So you can hurry to catch them. Éraste, good day!
(She exits.)

ÉRASTE:
Oh, heavens, how this long parade of pest and pestesss
Has ruined my day though I've done my bestest

To be with my beloved, my beauteous Orphise!
I'll follow her; I'll plead on bended knees.

(ÉRASTE *starts to follow* ORPHISE, *but* DORANTE *enters and latches onto him.*)

DORANTE: Marquis! Have you any idea how many
  pests surround us?
With each encounter, my own pleasures resound less!
And you see me just now in an enraged state,
Because an idiot—well, it's a story I must relate.

ÉRASTE:
I was just on my way to an earnest encounter—

DORANTE: *(Holding him back)*
You can hear my tale while together we saunter.
Just imagine! my hunting pals and I heard
Of a sixteen-point buck! That news lured
Us into thickest forest to sleep on the ground
And rise ready right at dawn. I have found
That true-blue huntsmen need no feathery bed,
But a small patch of grass and stars overhead.
We hunters slept well and then we ate
Some fresh eggs for breakfast on pewter plate.
The hounds were stationed in a well-chosen spot
By each *équipe*. Oh! it was Camelot!
Then what to my wondering eyes should appear
But a country bumpkin who'd heard of our deer.
He was, I'll allow, impressively mounted,
For I know horses—costly horseflesh, even discounted!
This poseur proudly presents a stupid chap, his son,
To join our hunt. I should have refused that one
Since the dog-horn he carried was the outmoded type.
His mangey curs he called "my pack"—such tripe!
Then we startle the stag and three leashes ahead
It leaps, our hounds follow. Mounted I sped—
I'd switched from my trotteur, a roan, to my chestnut.
You've noticed him, I'm sure.

ÉRASTE: I guess not.

DORANTE:
No! really? This Alézan's as beautiful as they come.
I bought him from Gaveau and paid a pretty sum.
It's a given that Gaveau keeps a first-rate stable,
But this swan-neck steed—I'm not able
To rhapsodize sufficiently. He's so noble, so fair.
His gallop's smooth and easy, more than any rocking
    chair!
Three hours pass quickly, then I see our stag on the
    run,
The cutter dogs cross ahead—but wait! there's more
    than one!
Our quarry, the quicker monster-antlered buck,
Lightly leaps a log, so graceful. Then, oh, f— bad luck!
The smaller-antlered beast attracts a part of my pack.
I sound my horn—Ta-rah!—to call them back.
But the ridiculous rustic blows louder to their
    confusion.
As if that's not enough, Sir, hang on for the conclusion.
After telling him off, with my dogs on I went.
We return to the woods and pick up the first scent.
Through brush and branches as thick as my arm,
We close in, the stag's at bay, my dagger out—and then
    wham!
A pistol shot! That fool! I'm enraged! I'm distraught!
Point blank to the forehead! Our entire hunt for
    naught!
The idiot shouts: "I've brought down our quarry!"
I want to strangle the boy, but I don't tarry
To lose my temper or do something to be sorry.
I turn and spur my horse and haste home without
    pause.
I'm still boiling over and now you know the cause.

[Upon entering, DORANTE *tosses his heavy musket for* LA
MONTAGNE *to catch and stagger under the weight. For his*

narrative, DORANTE *retrieves the firearm, aims it at* LA
MONTAGNE, *and motions for him to play the buck. This
becomes frightening on "my dagger out" and* ÉRASTE *jumps
up in anticipation of restraining* DORANTE, *who continues
his story, oblivious. After* DORANTE'*s exit,* LA MONTAGNE
exits as if running for the men's room.]

ÉRASTE:
Your restraint is admirable, and a hasty farewell
Is the best course with pests who make our lives a hell.
And so goodbye, sir,—

DORANTE: But we must chat again soon,
At a time and place apart from any peasant baboon.
(Exits)

ÉRASTE:
I'm losing patience, wanting just to gaze upon her eyes.
I'll kiss her little hands and, if need be, apologize.

(ACT TWO ballet)

First Entrée

(Some players of boule [bowls] stop ÉRASTE *to get him to
measure a distance under dispute. He gets away from them,
leaving them to dance the various poses typical of this game.)*

Second Entrée

*(Some boys with slingshots interrupt the players of boule,
but are chased away.)*

Third Entrée

*(Cobblers, male and female, their parents and others
interrupt but are driven away also.)*

Fourth Entrée

(A gardener dances solo and finally withdraws for the start of ACT THREE.)

[ÉRASTE exits, as three gardeners enter with watering cans. They share snuff in imitation of DORANTE's snuff-taking. Some male characters enter as dancers with large snapping fans for a rhythmic dance interspersed by moments of baroque elegance.]

END OF ACT TWO

ACT THREE

ÉRASTE: *(Ecstatic, addressing the audience)*
It happened offstage! We had a little *tête à tête.*
Sweet greeting and meeting! No need to fret
At my darling's discomposure. Orphise loves me yet.
Our hopes are now aligned but face a newer threat.
The worst of all the pests is her guardian, Madame
   Damis,
Who orders that Orphise be off-limits to me.
She forbids her niece to see me; she's made a plan
To betroth my beloved to some unnamed other man!
Happily, the renewed fond sentiments we expressed
Have given us both the courage to resist.
She'll let me into her lodgings for a secret rendez-vous;
More hurdles overcome mean more pleasures accrue.
Forbidden love is all the more to treasure and to prize.
It's nearly time. I'll go early to the one I idolize.

LA MONTAGNE: You want me to come?

ÉRASTE: Better not. There are some
Who would recognize you, and you'd flub playing
   dumb.

LA MONTAGNE: But, monsieur—

ÉRASTE: Enough! I'll slip in unattended.

LA MONTAGNE:
You know best, but best plans can fast be up-ended.

ÉRASTE: Must you eternally question my commands?
Oh, heaven grant me a valet who fully understands!

(Exit LA MONTAGNE. *Enter* CARITIDÈS.*)*

CARITIDÈS:
Monsieur, well met, though evening's upon us.
Morning's better for business, but it's a bonus
And an honor to speak directly with you.
Your social prominence keeps you well in view
But occupied, elusive, above scholars like yours truly—

ÉRASTE:
Monsieur, does some business pertain to me unduly?

CARITIDÈS:
Will your eminence kindly forgive my audacity
That impels me to implore in my humble capacity
This moment opportune—

ÉRASTE: Just say what you need to say.

CARITIDÈS:
Your rank, your renown, your riches hold such sway
In public opinion—

ÉRASTE: You're too kind, but I must go—

CARITIDÈS:
Monsieur, just a moment, it's awkward, I know
For you to deign to hear my self-introduction.
Please think me not lacking in social instruction.
I would prefer to meet you with all due formalities,
Credentials presented properly to put you at ease.

ÉRASTE: Sir, I can see you lack no social graces.

CARITIDÈS:
And I see all the virtues your kindness embraces.
That said, it is time that you learned my name,
Though my endeavors have not yet earned high fame.
Latin names are common. My Greek puts the stress
On the final syllable: I'm Monsieur Caritidès.

ÉRASTE:
Monsieur Caritidès, have you something else to do?

CARITIDÈS:
Let me read this letter written to the king. If you
Would convey it to him, I'd be much beholden.

ÉRASTE: Present it yourself. You can embolden
Yourself before him, as you've just done with me.

CARITIDÈS:
The king's open manner is known, but delicacy
Dictates my desire to have it reach his ear
When none else might be in proximity to hear.

ÉRASTE:
That can happen if you have the patience to wait.

CARITIDÈS: The truth is that palace guards abominate
Scholars and teachers; so does the public at large.
We're ill-treated, despised, and pushed to the marge.
Pursuit of knowledge makes us pursued in turn.
They'd like to throw us onto bonfires of books to burn.
If by your gracious hand this letter you'd deliver,
I could rest contented and in your debt forever.

ÉRASTE: Very well. Hand it here and I will do it.

CARITIDÈS: Here you are! But please first listen to it.

ÉRASTE: No—

CARITIDÈS: Really I could not ask you this favor
Without giving you the opportunity to savor
These noble thoughts to be conveyed to the king.
See if they don't have a strong resounding ring:
"To the king, Your Majesty, from your very humble,
very obedient, very faithful, and very, very studious
subject and servant Caritidès, French in nationality,
Greek in proclivity. Having observed the many and
serious abuses of language to be seen on signs and
placards in front of shops, taverns, inns, bowling
alleys and other places all over your beautiful city

of Paris, I dare to call the problem to your gracious
attention. Some of these signs use an apostrophe on
plural nouns when the simple S suffices. Some flout
correct usage of "its" the possessive pronoun and
"it's" as a contraction for "it is." Everywhere these
signs testify to a barbarous, pernicious, detestable lack
of intellect by misspelling common words with no
regard for etymology, analogy, or orthography. It's
an embarrassment to the republic of letters and to the
French nation when even drunken German tourists can
see these—"

ÉRASTE:
This becomes too long and some thoughts are repeated.

CARITIDÈS:
To be clear, Monsieur, not one word may be deleted.

ÉRASTE: Well then, skip to its conclusion.

[CARITIDÈS *begins unfolding an endlessly long missive, tries
to signal a paragraph in it, but* ÉRASTE *indicates "no". By
the time* CARITIDÈS *unfolds the letter to the conclusion, it
hangs down to his feet.*]

CARITIDÈS: "Your Majesty will benignly forgive this
intrusion, as I humbly supplicate for the good of the
state and the glory of his empire, that I be granted an
office of controller, intendent, corrector, revisionist,
and wordsmith-in-general to oversee the prolific public
placards of Paris. I further supplicate that I be honored
with appointment to this office in recognition of my
recognized attainments in learning, not to mention
services rendered particularly to Your Majesty with my
composition of anagrams of the words "your majesty"
in French, Greek, Latin, Hebrew, Syrian, Chaldean,
Arabic—"

ÉRASTE: *(Interrupting)*
That will do. Entrust it to me and be on your way.
The king will see your most unusual *dossier.*

CARITIDÈS:
Monsieur, I envision my dreams fulfilled without end
Once the king's eyes devour the words that I've
    penned.
As a token of my gratitude and high esteem,
I'll write you an acrostic if you tell me your name.

ÉRASTE: Farewell for now, Monsieur Caritidès.

(CARITIDÈS *exits.*)

ÉRASTE: Can learned men be such fools?
I fear for the generation in our nation's schools.

(*Enter* ORMIN.)

ORMIN: Monsieur, you suffered that dolt while the time
    I invested
Waiting till he left you has a value; you will be
    interested.

ÉRASTE:
I can't stay long. I've an appointment elsewhere.

ORMIN:
I'll bet you couldn't wait to get him out of your hair.
From the Marais to the Tuileries, he goes about
    critiquing
What he sees, buttonholing, always seeking
For his own advancement some kind of largess.
What good are scholars? I'm sure I can't guess.
But with me it's different, no fear of extortion;
I'm here, my dear Sir, to help you make your fortune.

ÉRASTE: This sounds like a sales pitch to desperate folk,
But our pre-capitalist age does not need to be woke.
Or do you trend to past ages and seek in time's mist
The philosopher's stone. Are you an alchemist?

ORMIN:
Ha! You've a fine wit and deserve a straight answer.
God keep me from alchemy—not a chance, Sir!
The deal I have for you, and through you, for the king,

Is a once-in-a-lifetime, grab-it-now sort of thing.
It's so special there are details I cannot yet divulge
Except to say it will make your biggest pockets bulge.
Mind you, I'm not meretriciously promising the moon,
But a steady flow of interest, risk free, and soon
If you care to buy in—

ÉRASTE: May we defer our conversation
To a later date? I profess another expectation.

ORMIN:
But you haven't heard the secret to financial winning.

ÉRASTE:
Please save it for later. My allowances are thinning.

ORMIN: Since you are first to know about my ingenious
   scheme,
If you'll lend me twenty écus, it's a sum you'll redeem
Many times over—

ÉRASTE: Willingly. Take this purse.
Farewell, Sir.

(ORMIN *exits.*)

ÉRASTE:
   Small change to buy my way away from pestly curse.
What a day! Too many pests! Am I finally liberated?
May I proceed to those delights so long awaited?

(FILINTE *enters, carrying two swords.*)

FILINTE:
Marquis, the news I hear brings me here at top speed.

ÉRASTE: What's this?
FILINTE:
         I'm your second—or any support you may need.
They say you challenged Alcandre, not without cause,
So I've rushed to—

ÉRASTE: I do not defy the anti-dueling laws.

FILINTE:
Your secret's safe with me, your devoted friend.

ÉRASTE:
Please will you bring that ugly rumor to an end?

FILINTE: You're here at dusk with no valet nearby.
It's clear it's an affair, no need to say why.
Your honor is mine, you should have sent word
I'm your man to second you, and here's my sword.

ÉRASTE: Won't you listen—

FILINTE: You wish to spare me, but no,
I'll stick with you, my friend, wherever you go.

ÉRASTE:
You've been duped by some gossip, it's malicious—

FILINTE:
To prove my loyalty to you I am always ambitious.

ÉRASTE: You really wish to oblige me?

FILINTE: Oh, Marquis, I do.

ÉRASTE: Then leave me this instant. I'm telling you true.
It's no affair of honor but an affair of the heart.
You know the court; our gallantry's an art—

FILINTE:
The more reason for me to remain by your side—

[ÉRASTE *takes the extra sword* FILINTE *was carrying and thrusts at* FILINTE's *feet, making him dance to avoid the sword thrusts.*]

ÉRASTE: It's too much! My rage is justified.
You won't listen; you hold out for action.
Then I'll give you lawfully spontaneous satisfaction.
Draw, sir, and we'll fight, you and me—

FILINTE: I want only to serve you. This cannot be.
Drawing on a friend is how you repay

My desire to serve? Then I'll be on my way.
(*He exits.*)

[FILINTE *flees the threat from* ÉRASTE'*s sword, but turns
back to pause at the exit for a courtly bow, which* ÉRASTE
reciprocates.]

ÉRASTE: We'll be friends again after you're gone.
Free at last! I'll see Orphise anon.
I'm late for my date with my little bonbon.

(MADAME DAMIS *enters and stands in the doorway.*)

ÉRASTE: But who—at her doorstep—or thereupon—?

MADAME DAMIS:
It's an outrage! To learn that he still plans to woo
Where I have forbid him. Oh, what won't I do—!

ÉRASTE:
It's her auntie, her guardian, who would foil our bliss
She blocks their doorway. What's now gone amiss?

MADAME DAMIS:
I've eavesdropped and learned that my deceitful niece
Plans to welcome Éraste inside. This must cease!

(*Enter* LA RIVIÈRE *and his* GANG, *making fierce noises.*)

LA RIVIÈRE: (*To his* GANG)
See that dame. I know her tunnel vision—
As if no one but her should get to make a decision.
She's one of them moralizers who's so hoity-toity.
Let's take her down—show how us guys can fight
    doity.

MADAME DAMIS: (*Seeing* LA RIVIÈRE)
You there, you want to earn some cash?
I need a few strong men to wait in ambush.
When ÉRASTE arrives, you'll all attack:
Knives, clubs, whatever, just drive him back.
His dogged persistence offends my honor.
I'll pay extra if—by your hand—he's a goner.

He fails to see failings in his ancestors' past,
While my own moral high ground has him outclassed.
He dares defy all that I deem is good,
So I seek satisfaction in his spilled blood.

[LA RIVIÈRE *and his* GANG *go into a huddle, making a
rumble of "rhubarb, rhubarb" sounds. Then they straighten
up to face her.*]

LA RIVIÈRE:
You're a fine one to try to tell us what to think!
What words we get to speak—it's over the brink!
Here's our game, guys, let's close in for the kill—

[LA RIVIÈRE *and his gang attack* MADAME DAMIS, *who
flees upstage and falls head over heels, white bloomers in the
air. She lies under her petticoats during the ensuing fight.*]

ÉRASTE: Madame Damis's my nemesis but honor
    impels me still.
I must rescue Orphise's auntie, it's only right.
Hold on, madame! To save you I'm joining the fight.

(*Brandishing his sword,* ÉRASTE *drives* LA RIVIÈRE *and the*
GANG *off stage.*)

[ÉRASTE *fights all* GANG *members at once in an impressive
display of swordsmanship. Two run and cower, but* LA
RIVIÈRE *disarms him completely. It looks bad for* ÉRASTE,
but suddenly LA MONTAGNE *appears, growling and
spinning his arms like a mad-man.* LA RIVIÈRE *is distracted
and* ÉRASTE *grabs his sword.* LA MONTAGNE *grabs the
saber, and all gang members are driven off stage.*]

MADAME DAMIS: What's happened? Who's saved me
    from certain demise?
Where's the hero? I want to reward and recognize—

ÉRASTE:
Madame, I acted only in the noble name of justice.

MADAME DAMIS: That voice! It's Éraste! Is it true—that
    this near miss—?

ÉRASTE: I'm truly happy I could be here to rescue
The source of my miseries, I confess you.

MADAME DAMIS:
I sought your death but see now I was wrong.
It's clear to me that we two can get along.
Your own extraordinary generosity
Quells my unwarranted animosity.
It's embarrassing to have taken a stance
That judged you wrongly without evidence.
Marquis, you are worthy to marry Orphise—

(ORPHISE *enters and runs to* MADAME DAMIS.)

ORPHISE:
Auntie, I heard some noise. Can you tell me, please—

MADAME DAMIS:
Dear niece, I have the joy and pleasure to report
That ÉRASTE was quick and brave enough to thwart
Some ruffians who would have slain me on this spot
And for my life I am ever in this man's debt.
If your hand in marriage might partially repay—

ORPHISE: Oh, yes!

ÉRASTE: Paid in full!

ORPHISE: When's the wedding day?

ÉRASTE: My heart is so full, after all I've been through,
Am I dreaming? Shall we have beer and barbecue?

MADAME DAMIS:
We'll have a properly French celebration.
Champagne and violinists are right for our nation.

(*Violinists, eager to play, knock loudly.*)

ÉRASTE: What's that clamor?

MADAME DAMIS:
                Our musicians want to join us on stage.
If we don't admit them, we'll hear unholy rampage.
A few violins, but mostly tambourines, rattles, and

drums
Learning to play together. The whole shebang—here it
  comes.

(*Dancers with mock instruments flood the stage and
surround the central characters.*)

ÉRASTE:
Pests! More pests! Let's away, Orphise, my sweet.
We'll leave the scene to the court and to their nimble
  feet.

(ÉRASTE *and* ORPHISE *exit.*)

(*ACT THREE ballet*)

First Entrée

(*Swiss guards with halberds chase off the pest-musicians and
leave the stage open for a dance by the company.*)

Second Entrée

(*Four shepherds and one shepherdess bring the musical
entertainment to a graceful conclusion.*)

[*All characters come on stage for a riotous dance. When
stately baroque music takes over,* MADAME DAMIS *leads*
ORPHISE *up center where* ÉRASTE *awaits alongside the
priest—*CARITIDÈS *in his academic robe—who will marry
them. During the bouncy French love song,* MOLIERE *enters
with a camera and photographs the wedding party, then
takes another as a selfie with himself in the foreground. This
segues into the dancing curtain call.*]

END OF PLAY

www.ingramcontent.com/pod-product-compliance
Lightning Source LLC
Chambersburg PA
CBHW070033110426
42741CB00035B/2758